T0145179

Tenacious Tori

Kelsey Kirk

To order additional copies of this book, contact:
Xlibris
1-888-795-4274
www.Xlibris.com
Orders@Xlibris.com

Tenacious Tori is such a tenacious little girl. She moves through a room with such a powerful whirl. It resembles a storm, a ruckus, a tornado that her parents have given her the name Torinado.

When she was little, her parents used to laugh that the Lord made her so quick and so fast. So head strong, no fear in her eyes. Like a lion, no place for worries to lie.

They knew there was a purpose, a purpose for this storm. They knew the Lord would use her in her ferocious form.

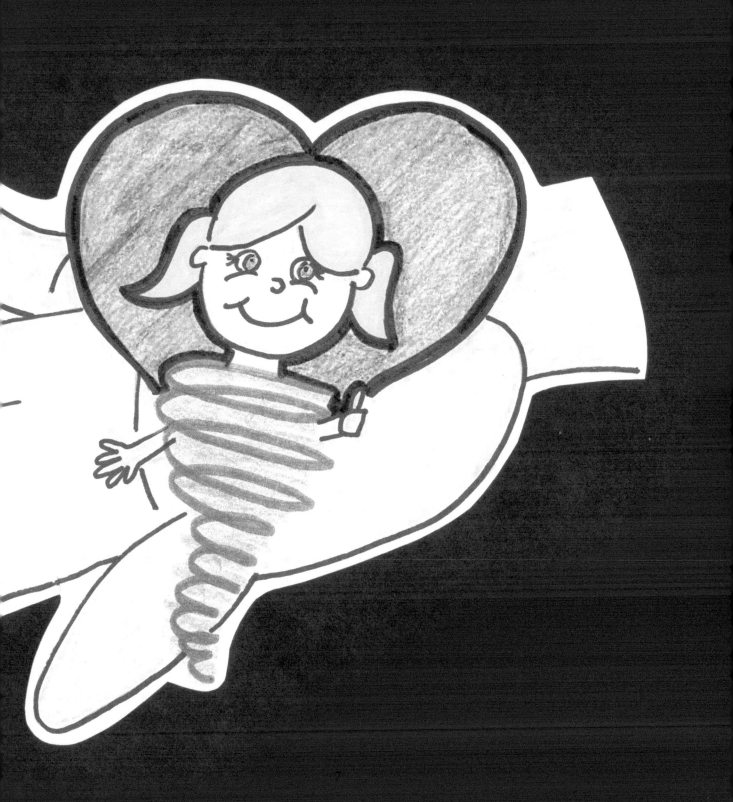

As she grew, so did her love for the Lord. As she grew, she used her storm as a sword. She was dressed in His armor, the armor of God. She traveled with His word. She took it abroad.

She moved like a storm, a ruckus, a tornado, that others around her gave her the nickname Torinado. She told everyone she met that the Lord loves them so. That He sent His only Son to die for their souls. That He is the way, and He is the truth. That He and His Son are Almighty. Yes, they are the fruit. That if only they call upon His Holy name, He is certain to love them, and sin He can tame.

Tori planted that seed that needs to be sowed. Tori helped it and watered it with His word, and God helped it grow.

Torinado was God's witness. She went without fear. Torinado was God's warrior. He loves her so dear. She is God's proof that He gives so perfectly, a gift to each of us that He chooses so carefully.

We should mold it and use it for His works alone. We should show it and share it and let it be known. Just like Tenacious Tori being such a tenacious little girl. That when she moved through a room, she moved with such a powerful whirl. It still resembles a storm, a ruckus, a tornado, and her parents still call her the name Torinado.

17

Printed in the United States
By Bookmasters